THE HORSE WHO
BEARS ME AWAY

poems

Jim Peterson

Red Hen Press | *Pasadena, CA*

Book design by Mark E. Cull

Library of Congress Cataloging-in-Publication Data

Names: Peterson, Jim, 1948– author.
Title: The horse who bears me away : poems / Jim Peterson.
Description: First edition. | Pasadena, CA : Red Hen Press, 2020.
Identifiers: LCCN 2020002070 (print) | LCCN 2020002071 (ebook) | ISBN
    9781597094115 (trade paperback) | ISBN 9781597098496 (ebook)
Subjects: LCGFT: Poetry.
Classification: LCC PS3566.E7693 H67 2020 (print) | LCC PS3566.E7693
    (ebook) | DDC 811/.54—dc23
LC record available at https://lccn.loc.gov/2020002070
LC ebook record available at https://lccn.loc.gov/2020002071

The National Endowment for the Arts, the Los Angeles County Arts Commission, the Ah-
manson Foundation, the Dwight Stuart Youth Fund, the Max Factor Family Foundation,
the Pasadena Tournament of Roses Foundation, the Pasadena Arts & Culture Commission
and the City of Pasadena Cultural Affairs Division, the City of Los Angeles Department of
Cultural Affairs, the Audrey & Sydney Irmas Charitable Foundation, the Kinder Morgan
Foundation, the Meta & George Rosenberg Foundation, the Albert and Elaine Borchard
Foundation, the Adams Family Foundation, the Riordan Foundation, Amazon Literary
Partnership, and the Mara W. Breech Foundation partially support Red Hen Press.

First Edition
Published by Red Hen Press
www.redhen.org

Acknowledgments

Bridge Eight: "Whatever," "Your Hand," "The Day of the Shark"; *Burnt District*: "New Animal"; *Carvings on a Prayer Tree* (a chapbook from Holocene Press): "Progress," "Old Listener," "Hunger in a Small Town," "Carvings on a Prayer Tree," "Wolf"; *Cave Wall*: "Mutation," "Full," "The Necessary," "Night, and the Mockingbird"; *Cream City Review*: "The Keys" (as "Empty Hands"); *Eclipse*: "Insomnia"; *Gargoyle*: "Dollars"; *Georgia Review*: "The Horse," "Rethink It," "The Hobo's Invitation," "The Mole"; *Georgia Review* (online), Dorine Jennette Continues the Conversation: "Masks," "The Brave," "The Radiance," "Why She Did It"; *Great River Review*: "Tundra," "Naked"; *Greensboro Review*: "The Origin of Mouths"; *I-70 Review*: "Blink," "The Ambush Garden"; *ISLE*: "Rain," "The Fall"; *The Literary Review*: "Breaking the Sage"; *Nexus*: "Progress," "Hunger in a Small Town," "Carvings on a Prayer Tree," "Wolf"; *Platte Valley Review* (online): "Salute," "Goya's Dog"; *Platte Valley Review* (print): "Sayings of an Old Slash Pine"; *The Poets Guide to the Birds* (Anhinga Press): "Listening to the White-Throated Sparrow"; *Poetry Northwest*: "Laid Off"; *The Point: You, Year: New Poems by Point Poets*: "This One Hat"; *roger*: "Manpower"; *Shenandoah*: "Breakfast at the Western Café"; *South Dakota Review*: "Open House," "Eternal House," "Study"; *Speech Minus Applause* (a collection from Press 53): "What You Know"; *Tar River Poetry*: "Spring on the Yellowstone"; *Tinderbox*: "Thin Air" (as "The Real Thing"); and *Town Creek Poetry* (online): "Signs."

For Harriet
and all the magnificent horses

For Patricia—new life

For my great friend
and beloved sister, Gayle

CONTENTS

❧ THE FALL / three / ❧

❧ ANYWHERE BUT OMAHA ❧

❧ MUTATION ❧

☙ EPILOGUE ❧

THE HORSE WHO
BEARS ME AWAY

It is not enough for a man to know how to ride;
he must know how to fall.

—Mexican Proverb

PROLOGUE

THE HORSE

In the enormity of bone and flesh
that splits the night with blood and breath;
in the rising brushstroke of pastern, fetlock,
cannon bone and stifle; in the rolling sloop
of dock, croup, withers and poll

I discover my body.
In the barrel that takes to the grip of thighs,
the flank that accepts the needling heel;
in the mane where I bury my hands at last;
in the forelock and muzzle of that long face;

in the chin groove, jaw and throat
that swallows my words like cracked oats;
in the two black eyes that glean the full circle
of horizon; in the shell-song of each ear;
in the heart, in the heart, the horse who bears me away.

THE FALL

/ one /

BREAKFAST AT THE WESTERN CAFÉ

Rain has muddied the river, someone says,
and spoiled the fishing for today.
Each day climbs on the back of the last one
like breath after breath getting nowhere.
The waitress at the Western Café,
blonde and beautiful and in demand,
turns that river of coffee
at the end of her hand
into cup after cup,
puts down a cinnamon roll
big as a boxing glove,
smiles over her secret frown,
and the long-faced rancher at table number four
will not look at her.
The girl who starts on Monday
sits at the counter all day
to learn the ropes.
For me this is time without encroachment
burning in my belly like a Mexican omelet.
A sign behind the counter says
"T-bone $2.95, with meat $8.75."
An old photo of the Roundup Parade from the Twenties
catches the marching band midstride,
sunlight flashing on the tubas and trombones.
Two guys remember the rumors of fraud—

a small boy creeping under the timbers
and the lazy sloshing of fire.
High on one wall the night-crawling skull of a steer
presides over this clanking of spoons and forks.
Everywhere here hands know their roles by heart,
curling over the edges of news,
drifting over food on grills and tables.
An old man in a small room adds receipts.
Hutterites at a long table behind me—
the strong, suspendered men,
the sackcloth, white-capped women—
laugh at their inside jokes.
Good workers, the waitress whispers,
but they'll steal you blind.
The cattle brands burned
into wooden plaques above our heads
roam over thousands of sections
on the butts of steers and cows.
The waitress goes home
where she chants in her children's ears:
smile, remember the regulars, keep moving,
there's always something needs to be done,
use up every second of your break.
Hearts that know their roles by hand
welcome exhaustion as a kind of peace.
An elk's head wears sunglasses, a white

Stetson, and a red bandana.
The bucked-off cowboy in an old photo
is always flying above that arched back—
glorious black oblivion in the horse's eye.

LAID OFF

Yesterday, I strolled among the cold meats
and the small bland vegetables in their bins
and could not find anything I wanted.
I admit, I took some pleasure in ramming

the metal cart into the long stuck row of others—
make of that what you will—and walked
into the street happy with my hunger.
I could feel my body retreating

into bone, my skin pulling tighter around me
in the wind. A seagull fed on tiny morsels
of something on the trashy asphalt,
a hundred miles from ocean.

Two miles away my wife was packing to leave me.
I left my car in the lot and walked into a neighborhood
among sparrows plunging their heads
into the blades of grass. Even the housecats

stretching and licking on windowsills
had something definite on their minds for later,
pausing mid-lick in case it might
be me, now. But today, I'll stay home,

making do with what I have. Outside,
everything is leaning into one
decision after another. A freight train
slows down to cross my street, one hand

emerging as if to wave from the long window
of a boxcar. In here, the fridge
is busy saving what is left of what is left.
The TV is a voiceless flickering in the corner

of my eye. Weeks ago I wrote the checks
for this brief future. Today I lie down
on the lawn I will not bother to mow again.

WHATEVER

I don't know why I always let them in.
Maybe it's the black spider tattoo
one skinny-ass boy flashes on his forearm.
Maybe I like these kids, maybe
I want them to like me,
an old out-of-work hod carrier
who once piled them into my truck
and took them to a movie about
getting revenge. I always ask, "What the hell
you doing down there in my basement?"
"Whatever," the one with a nose ring says,
shrugging his shoulders like someone
who once dreamed of throwing a ball.
"Old farts not invited," another one says.

I catch them tossing my hammers
like tomahawks at the old mattress
standing in a corner. Catch them
coughing up chunks of pot smoke
till they're looking at me from another planet
where laughing is the only form of speech.
Catch them playing with my antique guns,
my real-deal supply of black powder.
What the hell do they think it is,
something they can roll into a joint?

I'm sitting in my living room sucking
on beer #7, watching the best fighter
in the world pound-for-pound
beat some chump into a pulp,
when the floorboards fly up with a great
whump, an open fist of upright planks
and flying debris, one pine slab slamming
into the gimpy couch. I scramble
to a corner and curl up under a black cloud
raining socks and coins and crumpled cans—
and in the silence that follows
I watch a lamp in the shape of a dancing cat
my mother gave me years ago
slip into the crater of my living room floor,
hear it land like a brick in sawdust
somewhere down under, remember
the ornamental windmill she bought me
turning in my front yard among the weeds
pointlessly. I'm relieved. Now maybe
I can ditch this place she found for me,
set fire to that phony windmill while I'm at it,
spend my time somewhere my mother
can't find me honing the art of the left hook.
But I can't abandon these asshole kids
buried under my stupidity in the basement.

So I dig them out one by one,
their true parents in prison I heard
one say, or in rehab, or hiding
in a cold water duplex in the middle
of some nowhere I can understand.
I rub the dirt from their cheeks,
the blood from beneath their eyes,
drag them one by one out to the sidewalk
where they make a pretty row of ragged cigars,
still intact, still breathing, still dreaming
of a world that doesn't exist,
not even on TV.

YOUR HAND

wields mine
like a hammer
with nothing to strike

but the air.
The knot flung across
this city sidewalk

climbs and plunges
between us.
My hand says nothing

is happening here.
Enough, your hand
says, to stitch our

bones together.
Your hand is cold
and hard as a root—

mine smooth as a dust
jacket, warm as a woman
under sheets. Your eyes try

to capture mine, but I
focus on the street.
Your hand digs deeper

and says, *I'll work*
for food, I can clean
your gutters . . .

My hand coughs back
gotta go, gotta get
to the office, gotta call

my wife. Your hand
shrivels to a small fetus
that slips

from my grip
and flies down the street
at the end of your arm,

and I see you wholly now
as you turn to face the current
of pedestrians, buttonless

shirt, beltless old jeans,
the ripe fruit of your naked
feet, that same hand

reaching out, eyes
made strange by crazy,
relentless hope.

MANPOWER

This morning it's as dark outside
as the inside of a tire, and still I'm too late
to sit in one of these chairs

lining the walls and hooked together
like a chain-link fence. Steal one,
you steal them all. But I don't

need a chair anyway. A man
who carries nothing but himself
should not be sitting down. Better

to let the brothers and fathers
relax before they have to work.
I'll stand here beside

the water cooler, resting first one foot,
then the other, like an old horse
who has carried a thousand

children around a million circles.
The last time I held a child was 1975,
when my sister needed a hand

with Maggie, three years old.
I picked her up and those two big
blue eyes cut straight into me.

Oh Lord, how deep her eyes sank
into me. She never blinked, not once.
I had to set her down so I could trap

another breath and let it go. If only I
hadn't turned my back on her, to rest.
Her mother sauntered up wearing that Halloween

pumpkin hat she'd bought, carrying
a bag of carrots for the horse
she never rode—Maggie's absence

written on her face like a map
to nowhere. That's where Maggie was
all of a sudden: nowhere. I wish

I was a horse, beautiful, strong, instead
of this old carcass like a worn map
to the edges of nowhere safe. Oh Lord.

I think I'm going to just stand here
with all the rest of the late arrivers until
my number's called and somebody

gives me work. Anything, the heavier
the better. I may look old, but I
can still throw a load over my shoulder.

Robert Mitchum did that in a movie once
with a woman, till he lowered her
kicking into a great river where they

laughed and splashed. Rich.
I don't mean to say I'm such
a man. Whatever they give me

to carry, I can embrace it like a sack
of Idaho potatoes, all those eyes
hidden away, like the hands
of children on a very cold day.

INSOMNIA

is a small child turning round and round
with her arms outstretched,
fingers testing the air.
Her spinning is a kind of waiting
for the man to stir. He sits at a desk,

dozes on his hands, stumbles
through half-dreams about his late wife
and their stillborn child.
The girl has come this far many times
for many years,

turns and turns searching
for a crack in the man's dream,
has a word for the man.
He cannot sleep in his bed,
cannot plan on sleep, cannot let go

and pass over, can only fall
mid-sentence mid-act
into the shallows.
She can come in this moment only,
her mind a spun bell,

her painted toes twisting
on carpet, thin body whirling and whirling,
her face a veil of flying hair.
He waits in his dream for her arms
to drop at last at her sides,

for her body to crystallize,
disheveled hair still concealing her face.
She smiles, he thinks as he wakes, she brushes back
her hair to reveal the bell of an eye,
or is it a word unintelligible
ringing in the empty room?

THE HOBO'S INVITATION

sit down and have some cheese
nobody else is coming for dinner
I can't tell you that God is not love
but I can tell you the rain comes down again
and finds every crack in this roof
my leg swells up again like the river
the mice watch every move we make
cell phone towers are milking the air
the cost of living is having to eat this damn cheese
on this night when the moon won't show its face
that mockingbird doesn't ask a single question
just makes pronouncements in every language known to bird
probably thinks this cheese would taste good
look at that dollar on the table unfolding
stretching its legs like it owns the place
the dimes whisper to the nickels in rhymes
gotta keep our light small so nobody'll see us
far above us in the dark the cold fog
tumbles down the mountain
we can travel unseen in the morning
I'll show you how to find the right train
how to be a shadow among the other shadows
what's the use of preaching
tried that for about ten years
still don't know what a soul is

what's the use of knowing anyway
even the lies are a kind of knowing
water's come through this room before
look at those boards all twisted and warped
all the trees had to swallow hard that day
orange juice would taste good right about now
real cold with the right amount of pulp
bears are showing up in the neighborhoods
the grasshoppers died off or flew away
to follow the signs like a real man would be a mistake
to remember the museum dummies is foolish
Daniel Boone reloading his long rifle
Sitting Bull passing the pipe
got my own damn pipe and a little bit to smoke
you can have some if you like it
makes the cheese go down easier
that tie of yours would make a good belt
that ring you got on your finger's gonna disappear
into the thinnest air you've ever breathed

THIN AIR

for Ed Arnold

1.
A blond patch of hair
sprouts at one end of the bed,
the sprawled length of his body
twisting in the sheets,
the hard round knot of a muscle
in the folded rope of an arm,
the fine-boned sculpture of his face,
eyes the blue of clear water.
How can a mole on his back, he asks,
keep him home and in bed
on this luminous day?
That cagey version of his tenor voice
shifts into things about girls,
the things we will want to do
when we're old enough to have
the real thing.

2.

His grin flashes a major set of braces.
He searches for a teammate to pass to,
but the defense has all of us covered.
So, alone and deep in the corner,
his bony length rises from the floor
in a jump shot,
for a moment graceful in the air,
feet flopping, head cocked,
ball perched above the sweaty palm,
then rolling off the fingers,
spinning away from the wrist's release
into the bold stroke of an arc—
the ball dropping into the waiting net
like a stone into water.
It holds there for an instant
as his body in the corner
holds its form in the air
before sinking back to the floor
and turning away with a fist-shake and a shout—
back a patchwork of tape and gauze.

3.
And so the lumps reappear on his back
and the women cry in shifts
in a room far away from his
while the pain uncurls,
lengthens like a whip to crack
the tired horse of his brain.

4.
The unfamiliar trim and stiff training of his hair
makes him look butch like the fifties, or the army.
The sheet offers in relief the frailty of his body.
His eye lies still beneath the lid.
Stringing his fingers with hers
in a kind of cat's cradle
she hums a gentle song for sleeping children.
She holds a cup and straw before him
caring how she moves his "lazy head."
He sucks the Coke
into the stillness of his throat
where it holds for a moment
till she strokes and coaxes
and the swallow slides down like an egg.
When she tells him in a rising tone
who has come to see him
he lifts the little finger on his left hand
and lets it drop again.
He knows who you are, she says,
he knows you are here.

THE FALL

/ two /

RAIN,

your voice filters down to me
through cottonwood leaves,

strokes me into quiet gray
light under the window,

crawls shaggily into my ear
like a late fall fly. You would

confine me to the room of my
own song, but I will not give you

the satisfaction. There is nothing
in my hands on the table.

I step outside and catch
your slang on the brim of my hat.

Your words have taught me
to search for the small dry

underside of an alder leaf
where the wolf spider sleeps.

I have learned to follow
the syntax of your falling,

your parallel structures
tumbling over the ground

to the place where I belong.

TUNDRA

For more than one year
I have wanted to talk to a crow.
Coming down the Beartooth Pass today
I spotted a giant one, a raven maybe,
ranting on the dead limb of a tree
on the low side of the road.
No one was in my rearview mirror
so I stopped and rolled down my window.
With each embellishment
he dipped his head and lurched,
the whole tree twisting in a mad loop.
He spoke to someone on the high side
above my head out of sight and ignored me.

"What are you doing?" I said.
He stopped his exclaiming to look at me.
"What are you doing? What are you doing?"
I was in a great mood from hiking
fifteen miles of Beartooth tundra.
I never thought he would look at me,
but he did, for five seconds, maybe six,
his eyes black beetles in the sun.

He was so black the light loved him
and fell from his back like thrown knives
bouncing off a rock.
"What are you doing? What are you doing?"

I could see in his eyes
he knew who I was exactly.
"Stupid human," he said,
then lifted from that limb like a helicopter
from the chaos of a battlefield—
filled beyond capacity
with the wounded and the dead.

PROGRESS

Paved roads rebel,
buckle in their narrow paths.

There are plenty of full tanks,
millions of tires,
but the cars are part
of this refusal,
come to rest in fields,
doors swung open,
dome lights growing dim.

The houses have already
dragged themselves
like turtles into the sea.

The groan of homes breaking away
from foundations
tore us all from the last good sleep,
the last good meal.

At first we wielded guns
but when we laid them down
they burrowed into the ground like moles
and disappeared.
Now,
no sound is noise only.

Movement is useless.
It is the same everywhere.
Silence travels faster than news,
descends on us like the air itself,
like the woods growing dark around us.

THE FALL

In the woods I touched a tree
thick and tall with age,
scarred and dark.
I heard the sharp
scratch of claws, caught
the cold scent of blood.

I climbed out of sight of ground
toward a black cloud
trapped in leaves—
a porcupine grown big as a black bear.
The tree's crown flared
above its head. Concealed

by canopy,
it stripped off and ate
the green bark of new growth.
Its yellow-tipped hair
glistened in the spare rays of the sun.
And beyond, the long body of a cougar

with eight quills in its throat
dangled in a net of limbs.
I fell from the tree—
lay stunned among roots and stones—
a man staring up
into the face of innocence.

SIGNS

They nailed their placards
to the trees, men who
stumbled over spoken words
as children do when on display.

Such messages drew the ire-sap
of Madam Leaf. So she turned
men's thoughts into dragonflies
cruising the black swamp at dusk,

their dreams into the blasted hearts
of chicadees roosting in a scrub-oak
ditch, the dark matter of their deep
sleep into small, rabid lizards

clinging to the screens of closed
windows. Moons rose on posted
blurbs. Windy rain smeared words,
meanings tied to a single day.

When pruners came to take out
limbs for their high wires
full of signs, Madam Leaf turned
into a girl no more than twelve

but strong as a same-aged oak.
She told a fable in the air with only
the numberless lobes and teeth
of her fingers. The spell

of her unspelled words rattled
the locked doors of stories
old as the dawn, old as the silence
before voice. Axe handles fell

to ground, struck roots like saplings
deep into fissures. Blades
relaxed into random stones.
The girl's face flickered in the glade.

SPRING ON THE YELLOWSTONE

Early wind, the loose pane rattles. Already
killdeer feign injury in the grass. Rimrock
junipers crouch and lean. The river,
clotted with the deadfall of cottonwood,
mounts its own carved banks.

Your bare foot flattens on the icy floor,
pokes the fetal ball of your dog.
You buckle the cold around your waist,
pull it over your head, whistle it into windows.
By mid-morning, rattlers lie like frets across the trail, owls

like blinking whole notes on the limb above you.
The she-bear shambles through your camp
with her cub in tow. The ground plunges
into gorges, clambers back up into sage.
Then the afternoon light lies down on the wrack

until it breaks. Something not water courses
down the canyon. Later, you smell the river flooding—
cold-blooded brother of night—and drive to where
the blacktop crumbles. There, a horse borne away
by high water neighs to the sky, and goes under.

CARVINGS ON A PRAYER TREE

Under the moon and sun,
under the leaves, under the clouds,
me. And the grass is under me,
alive like the skin of a dog,
and the night is waiting in the windows
for us all
to come in.

⚘

I would vote for the sun.
I would vote for the hours like days.
I would make my mark by the wind
giving it its head,
and the animals would make their own marks
out there in the night
that does not need my vote.

⚘

I believe in speech
and the isolation of each word flying off
like shavings from the blade
and the cohesion of those words
in what remains

like the stillness of limbs
after sleep,
the slow fire in a cell.

❧

I could have been born in the right place,
not here where the hours
cluck around in the yard,
but solidly there among the doors,
among the lights coming on and going off.
I would've promised not to say anything,
not to emerge among others
as a presence to be reckoned with.
The day grows hot in my feet and hands.
The trees touch the high air
and gather the rain shaking it down.
The wind is rude as always.
Every moment I wake up right here,
oh Lord secretive as the hopes of trees,
and always someone is approaching.

❧

Called out again,
taken by the hand and drawn into eyes,
again I am feeble,

my words the same old cold chips.
They bring me children
who could be anybody.
They say make them into somebody,
they say show them how the halls
turn and ascend.
All day I stand among the seated.

ℐℓ

My face is beside me on the pillow,
its eyes are open,
its lips parted.
It is not waiting for anything.
Again it has forgotten my name
as in an hour of deep sleep
I will forget this moment.
It shines, it is not a mask,
it is empty as a rose.

ℐℓ

First light in the window
I see a man on a roof
testing himself at the edge.
He reaches out to a limb

and leans across.
All the senses rise up in the fingers of my right hand
and in my palm
that one
that holds them all together.
I can feel the others in the growing light,
still asleep,
coming part way to themselves.
How do we connect?
We lean, catch hold and swing out.
It is the same tree,
it is the same wind beneath our feet.

♉

Maybe I can find a place in the forest
where the light breaks through,
and I can lie on the pine straw and last year's leaves
drawing a cocoon of warmth around me
and feel again that I am alone.
The palm of my hand molts and tumbles off among the leaves.
My names relax their hold like hair
and fly off over the ground among roots,
and the hours settle down on my body
and lay their eggs in my veins.

Set me down in another day, Lord.
Though this one is still bright and beautiful as the eye of a storm,
I see the end of it
hatching out in the faces all around me.
I turn toward these faces
but can never touch them.
I can hold my words out on a plate
but there is no nourishment in them.
The day is half done
but I am still wiping
the sleep from my eyes.

THIS ONE HAT

One day warm air will blow in
from a dangerous place,
and the shovels will shake
free from the walls,
soot will bake into the worn handles,
and believers will still huddle under the trees
along the back roads of the valley.

I will understand for the first time
the old lessons
sleeping in new graves,
footprints brushed away by leaves,
the lowliness of water,
and a dream of unknown faces
will attach itself to my hands,
their persuasions
dropping like small white stones
to the natural grass, to the weeds.

When all the deadlines have passed
I will not hide in the shadows
of remembered days.
I will lay the old knowledge aside
and hold onto this one hat,
this one pair of shoes.
I will make them last.
I will pass the half-open doors of the old

hoping for a visit from lost friends,
the raised windows of the young,
the torrent of their music
overwhelming the cries of cicadas.
I will pass the turned backs of the rich
behind their walls and gates,

the turned back of the rain
as it moves away through trees,
light beginning to crawl out
from the roots
with the soul of a man.

THE DAY OF THE SHARK

Maple leaves. One lies
on my living room floor,
dragged in through the dog door
by the puppy, no doubt;
another spread-eagled on the front porch
as I step out to get the paper.

Bad news today: a shark
ate a girl's arm while she swam
too far out from the shore
of Myrtle Beach—forever less now,
somehow forever more, learning
to garden with one hand, intimate

now with the cold, beautiful
death-smell of blood in the water.
Another leaf on the sidewalk
straddles the crack between two
concrete slabs. At least one maple lives
in every yard of my street,

making the history of rakes
and wind, of great shadows
cooling our houses against the sun.
This time of the year, vast herds
of the fallen—red and yellow—graze
in the underbrush of woods that begin

at the end of my block, turning life
into death and back into life again
and again like everything else that lives.
I just keep walking and reading
about that one-armed girl, and when I get
back home and turn the key in my lock,

as if something worth protecting
lurked within the walls of my old house,
a maple leaf stuck by the damp breeze
on the windowpane of my door
throws its truncated, serrated arms back
in strange hilarity, shouting in its veiny silence:

"Wake Up! Wake Up! Wake Up!"

THE FALL

/ three /

BLINK

From rice fields
to the black roots of stars,
from the blaze of rails
to the beaten air of wings,
breathes the same old disappearing act:
listen to every unlikely leaning,
says the man clinging to the top of a ladder,
to every melodramatic degree of moon,
says the woman lying on her back
in the midnight grass. Everything
is good, the gutter man says,
every torn bit of leaf, broken twig,
every lick of rain over shingles.
We are all the same and we all die,
says I, but we have learned to dream,
to hang on every shred of cloth
that has ever touched our skin
as if it told some unforgivable
yet exciting sin. Have learned, more
importantly, to piss in the yard at 2 a.m.
while neighbors turn over and over
in their white sheets under the sizzling
hiss of streetlights. Have learned
to seek out one forbidden bliss after another
until our faces disappear before our eyes,
our hands, our feet, our genitals

grown lonely in their dark folds.
And we suspect you as the source
of our losses, original blankness,
blink of blackness under the laugh,
shin bone half-submerged in sand.

DRUNK TANK

How many times? the cop asks. He closes
handcuffs behind my back, pushes my head
down, forces me into the steel mesh cage
of the back seat. I say, I don't know, and he says,
Well, they're gonna charge you with assault
this time. Oh yeah? I say. Yeah, he says,
you could see jail time, and I say, Big deal.
Later, at the jail, I try to elbow him
as he unlocks the cuffs. I spit at him.
Tough guy, he says, and shoves me in. I take
a swing at his face, but my broke hand hits bars,
and the pain shoots through me like electric shock.
The cop laughs with those same eyes.
Those fucking eyes are everywhere.

A man wearing a red cap knocks me down
with one punch. His friends join in—kicks
to the stomach, stiff jabs to the back of my head,
but their hearts aren't in it, they know I'm just
one of them. My bottom ear mashed against
the cold concrete hears as if through sloshing
water . . . a voice like a distant bass playing scales,
but I can't make out the words. My top ear
opens wide as if to let in a swarm of shouts
like a party on a summer beach a mile away.
I remember that someone is looking through these eyes,

feeling the pain of these arms bent and these hands
twisted against this back, this face trying to hold
a Mister Cool expression, untouchable smirk.

Someone sits down on me. A herd of scuffed shoes
rumbles by. Someone yells, Fuck you,
and red-hat guy takes him down with the help
of his pals, a muffled quiet to keep the guards
away while they kick him in the gut and face.
Not too much, just enough to shut him up, a mist
of burned out love hanging in the air above them.
Here I am again, flattened on the cold floor,
wrestling with my death wish—but no, he's real,
I can smell his whiskey breath, feel his calloused
hand, his heavy butt cheeks pressed against my back.

The other knocked-down man looks at me
across thirty feet of frozen concrete tundra,
his dark eyes full of wonder and shame. Some big,
blasted kid sits on him, dreaming of being red-cap guy
when he grows up. I look into the other sap's eyes
that know me like the shit-mud he rose up from.
And I know him too, from the night-street,
or from some lowdown bar. Blood drools from his lips
but still he begins to shape words. They tumble
like weeds across this concrete plain and prick

my face. Raise hell, he says, until it burns the sky.
Kick ass because you feel like it, because something
in the world ain't right, because eyes and voices
oughta know respect. Go fuck yourself, I say,
and those words feel good coming out of my gut.
I like to feel the body of my voice like this,
hard and aimed to hurt like a thrown rock. Bravo,
the other man says, blowing bubbles of blood.
They sent me, he says, and I have to do whatever
they want, I have to rip out your heart and throw it
in the river. You can try, I say, and the lights flicker.
In a flash, it's just him and me in this empty room
circling each other like a pair of enemy kids.
I am your other self, he says, your father, the one
who has beaten you to a pulp a hundred times.
And yet I come back for more, I say.

Eras pass, continents shrink and disappear
or rise up from ocean floor. Where monsoons
pounded the land for months, deserts
return heat to naked sun. Lizards slither
into shadows of rocks. And when I wake,
white light burns my eyes. Blood pours out my face
onto his that I hold in my hands. You win, he says,
his voice a razor in my head. It's all yours, he says,
What are you gonna to do with it? Before I can

answer, he crumbles under my fingers, his particles
scuttling away like the night roaches
in this old jail. In a moment I'm alone on the floor
with just the feet of other drunks, my other self
so far gone now I can't believe my luck, his particles
of thought-dust flying toward the barred moon.
I crawl to my corner and sit down. Still, someone
is looking out of these eyes. Who is it this time?

The one who only sees? The one who becomes
what he sees? The one who sees only what he believes,
who sees only the history of what he's already been?
Suddenly, someone calls my name. My sins
have been paid for. A guard swings
the steel door open for me, and I see my daughter
faraway down the hall, silhouetted in a doorway,
so young and beautiful and worthy of a good man.

But I can't leave now, when the party is about to begin
for real. I stand up and spread my blood-spattered coat
wide like a matador's cape. Seeing nothing but red,
one by one the drunks—carpenters with
cracked hands, clerks with pale faces
and wire-rimmed glasses, garbage men
with long hair and ancient boots—charge,
their hand-horns ripping out pockets and inseams,

scattering wadded up cash and bar nuts, slips
of paper with numbers and names—Julie, Elizabeth—
and crumpled business cards—insurance agents, oil
changers, poets, barbers—none of them my own.
My daughter shouts for me to come home,
but I ignore her—a habit of many long days
in the spirit of the father I once knew.

All night they are the bulls and I am the matador,
stabbing their necks until they can no longer
lift their heads, no longer stand, no longer focus
on anything but their own miserable selves
like this battered, gray, concrete floor. Still,
I take up cape and lance and provoke
each one of them to stomp his feet and fight again.
I have to kill every last one of them before I leave.
How those ruined particles of love-dust scream
in their tiny voices as they fly away, how the crowd
tears their shirts off and waves them, and the moon
in the window hangs fat and yellow, so low,
and so desperately round.

THE MOLE

I am the fox that listens to the mole,
or the mole, something in me says, that reveals
its ancient goal. I wish I could say
I have let go of the whiskey, the pot, the bad
politics, my dream of a loving and available

god. How can I convince myself of my own
worth standing knee-deep in the creek
like all the other stones, or lying back
in the driver's seat in an empty parking lot
watching the weather through curved glass?

I still look for the light in myself and others—
the gang of boys cruising on their skateboards,
the homeless old dog scavenging the cracks
and curbs, trying to remember that warm
corner where he curled up last night. I feel

for the pistol my father left me 35 years ago,
unfired in all that time, the ammo almost
as old as I. If that man creeping around
the closed grocery store approaches me, I'll just
give him what I have: a few bucks, my old

pair of boots still waterproofed. But nobody
heads in my direction. Maybe we all understand
each other, or maybe I'm scary as hell,
a tuft of my hair visible in the half-lowered window.
Maybe they can sense that .38 curled up

like a small, cold cat in my coat pocket.
I hope not. I don't mean to have it. I just do.
I've decided I don't need to understand
anything. I'll just lie back in the creek and allow
the water to flow over me. I was falling asleep

anyway, not waking up, as I had hoped.
I've decided to be the contented mole
traveling underground, pushing up
circuitous mounds to draw the hungry fox,
to be this old man half asleep, half

awake, sitting in his beat-up car, the given
swirling around me like the glints of light
on a summer lake, the all-consuming,
unimportant journey still coursing through me
like the dream I almost forgot, but didn't.

ANYWHERE

BUT OMAHA

RETHINK IT

Rethink the way your feet hit the ground, the way the left one flattens out, too straight to be agile, the way the right one curls like a leaf in a fire, jumping quick in a gust of wind.

Rethink the blues, the way you ask for them, a man who settles for the corner table with a bitter beer, the way you fall into lockstep on the dance floor, loving your misery, the swirls of smoke coalescing into the woman you remember in some doorway, on some corner, in some dream that only starts and never ends.

Rethink the eyes in the moon with the clouds flying over them like crumpled silk sheets.

Rethink the game, the way the rules keep you from running fast, or from walking so slow even the trees grow rings of envy.

Rethink your house—yes, the one where you curl up like some gopher in its hole, the way it smells like an old you, the way it lets the light in just right so that it doesn't touch the skin of your arm, your foot, your belly rising and falling to the tune of a recurring dream where you learn to make plates, the same plates, over and over.

Rethink the way you smile, mouth's corners twitching with effort, lips stretching to the split point in dry weather, eyes going soft and buttery, as though you're some sort of spread waiting for the right piece of bread.

Rethink the way your hands shape and hold the space around you, that shallow space you breathe in where your eyes construct their lines of sight to the same bricks, the same crumbling sidewalk, the same white doors and creaking floors where the same voices speak of the same matters, the ones that don't matter.

Rethink your thoughts just to see them running in circles like mice crazed by irrelevant shocks. Open the cage door and watch them run out into grass among the roots and dogs and cats. Let them go.

Rethink thinking—it belongs to you. You can hold this thought like a man who makes his own sandwich, who takes a step toward the woman he wants to meet, toward a lake in warm weather where he can strip down and dive in.

Rethink the sandwich, the way the tomato is falling out the side, the way the mustard requires more attention, the way the slices of turkey remember their integrity among the low-hanging limbs, the way the lettuce funnels drops of water into the bread, onto the counter, the napkin. Rethink the sandwich altogether. Peanut butter. Pimento cheese. Chicken salad. Stop thinking. You know what you want. This voice is you thinking. Is that what you want? Is it?

MASKS

1.

The skin of my face takes the shape of each outward attitude I
need, like the one for her after I ran away because I was scared
of a strange man on our street and she found me huddled in
the woods and pressed her hand on my chest to feel the rattling
of my heart; like the one for him when I came home when I
wanted to, which was way late, his hand unbuckling the belt
and whipping it from around his waist, throwing out and
uncoiling that black circle of himself until the backs of my legs
gave up every last hope of ever sleeping and forgetting; like the
one for those who gave me a place in the crowd at school to hide
when I didn't know who I was or what I was or where I might
possibly go; like the one for her whose eyes shone through her
mask to something in me that she saw and liked that I didn't
know was there but now I do; like the one for sky with white
clouds passing over, black clouds passing, clear sky full of the
mask of the sun pretending to be nothing and everything at
once; like the one for catching rain and letting it in, the one
for making a speech, the one for shaking hands; like the one
designed to fit snugly in the palms of my hands when I need
to hold it, to feel its exterior separateness, to feel through it
inwardly toward a position that witnesses all of my masks and
looks out through their eyeholes, seeing that deep witness in
others that lives and understands from a place beyond the need
for masks.

2.

What means to you a mask? the shaman asks, sitting on the floor
cross-legged behind a small altar holding stones and feathers.
I make them for money, she says, *I create them to stay alive, to
hold my dream faces in my hands, my powerful faces that cause
the world to give and take.* He says, *hmmm, that's interesting.* She
says, *I make them to sell in gift shops and galleries, all of my faces
going out into the world and possessing the others, covering them,
mastering them, becoming them, until I can take my mask off and
lay it in the grass and walk away like it's just another leaf that let go,
blowing in the wind, flying over the shoes of strangers, disappearing
in the woods where the deer curl up and sleep at night.* He says,
hmmm, I understand.

He begins to rattle and sing, calling to the beings of light, the
spirits of the sacred mountains, the condor and the puma, the
being of the plant medicine that pulses green and shining in his
veins. She falls, as if something is guiding her down, her body
collapsing like a segmented tent pole but stretching out again
on the floor. The shaman goes to her, strokes the long Condor
feather over her again and again, flicking the tip as it passes
over her feet. He keeps singing and shaking his rattle, and her
body stretches and stretches and flows like the part of a river
seen through a gap in the leaves. She is the river of masks. She
is the mask of the one river always changing.

THE BRAVE

A man sat down in his favorite chair. He was good at doing. He
had made a complete study of his usual doings as he was doing
them and he had discovered that they were as automatic as the
rinse cycle of a washing machine or the bark of a dog. The man
felt himself become very still outwardly. Inwardly he fell deeper
into a well of letting go. He fell for a long time, letting go of
every single thought and feeling and thing. He arrived at a quiet
place where he could hear only his breath. He followed it with
the same fascination with which he once watched the rolling in,
the breaking, the unraveling of a wave onto shore, then the way
the energy turns and withdraws into the great body, the way
it turns again and curls up on itself way out there and starts
back in. The man found the space in time between the uprising
of the breath and the downward falling of it. This space was
an emptiness that he could occupy, and he did, slipping in at
the last second like a dog through the closing crack of a door.
He felt himself in a room that was expanding, swirling with
an inflowing energy like wind that nourished his awareness of
himself. He felt more and more there.

The energy spun upright into a woman made of wound strings
of light. When she spoke, the man felt her voice at the top of
his head, a spiral of energy running down into all of the centers
of his body, lighting them up one by one. He stood on a height
from which he overlooked the universe of himself, vast and full
of light. His body was sitting still in the big chair in his study.

But his other body stood as witness to galaxies. The woman said, "Now return to your old self, your body sitting in that chair far away. But you must also remain here. Only the bravest can go and stay at the same time." He stood up from the chair, walked outside, stared at the night sky, feeling the galaxies resonate deep inside.

THE RADIANCE

Each day, as she stepped from the light of the street into the
darker realm beneath canopy, she felt she was entering a body.
She had seen a map of this forest with its cold-water creek
meandering at the bottom of a ravine, its rolling upper slopes
of old oaks and maples and sycamore, its groves of cedar and
loblolly pine. The map showed her the true shape of her friend,
limbs extending for miles between subdivisions and even to
the edges of town, though most people paid no attention to it,
too rugged and steep at the center to be developed, forcing the
town to build bridges and bypasses. The heart of these woods
lay deep in the ravine where the creek pooled and gathered
light from the ribbon of sky. The homeless sometimes made
camp here. But she almost never felt afraid in the woods. She
strolled, took in the fragrance of leaves, sometimes lay down in
the path and spread her arms wide, as if to embrace the forest,
or straddled a low limb like the back of a horse and gazed over
the spangled hills like some new kind of animal. Still, she was
frightened on some days, sensed someone watching her.

One day, she heard a movement behind her. She stopped
and did a spinning jump, shouting "Hah!" as her feet landed
shoulder-width on the trail. She kept her knees bent, her
hands in fisted readiness, but nothing was there. She felt it
behind her again and repeated the maneuver, to discover only
the familiar trail. But a presence hung so close that its breath
hovered around her face like smoke in a bar. She continued to
walk. The being moved all around her and gathered on her skin;

as she relaxed, it followed the inward path of her letting go. She allowed it to enter and to fill her. Her body glowed in the dim, afternoon light of deep forest. She turned her attention to a tone that hummed in her bones like a plucked string, a sound that meant she would never sleep again.

She liked her sleep, she liked her dreams, but the presence told her they had to change. She unfolded the leaves of her holding-on like money from a thick roll of bills and paid them out to the presence, one at a time, until none were left and her hands and her mind were empty. The white flowers of a lone dogwood captured the light, razor sharp, of an early moon. A pair of woodpeckers called to each other and she caught a red glimpse of them flying from limb to limb. She sat down at the foot of the tree, took a deep breath, realized she no longer knew what to do. She had never really known. She sank down into the cocoon of not knowing for a long time, feeling her body merge with the tree and the spiraling-upward reach of its sap and leaves.

Much later, her house, no more than a mile away, called to her. The old cat, curled up on the red cushion of a chair, awaited her evening meal. The moon reached down through the canopy and revealed the faint rambling of the trail. The woman walked, knowing only the sensations of her living skin in the night air. Finally, she found an opening and stood at the edge of woods looking out on the street where she lived. Her neighbor's children screamed and laughed on their lawn. She pushed against a pressure like a membrane of air, and broke out of the woods onto the grassy bank of her street. That night, she grew weary as always, and she slept, but a part of her remained awake. She entered her dream as if it were the body of a forest. Her radiance reached and reached until it touched someone out there in the distance: a woman on a horse flickering in and out of sight among the trees.

WHY SHE DID IT

She did it because she'd carried me for all those months until
her legs and feet were so swollen she could hardly cut herself
loose from the moorings of the bed and drift to the kitchen,
where she cooked another meal for everybody. My daddy sat
at the table in his sport coat, tie loosened and a hunger raging
in him that fried chicken and mashed potatoes and sweet tea
and two daughters and a boy on the way and his wife floating
into the dining room with serving bowls like a Macy's parade
balloon would never satisfy.

She did it because she didn't know me and never would, the
way things were going. She knew the one who wore a suit and
tie and stood where he was supposed to stand at my daddy's
funeral, but that wasn't me, the real me inside hanging on to
the face of a cliff thousands of feet above the boulders of a river,
trying to pull myself up to some ledge where I could catch
my breath and sit down and look through my eyes for a few
minutes without feeling like I was going to fall.

She did it because she'd sold the house and paid the bills
and had enough left to carry on for a little while if she didn't
have to drag her big boy with her every step of the way. Meaning
me. She told me once that I'd never know what it had cost her to
get me outside her body. She had paid and paid. Because I was
the last one, the one she'd fought for because she wanted a boy
for my daddy, a handle on the life she was making that he could
hold onto. He had a strong grip when he wanted to use it.

She did it because she had a full tank of gas in a beat-up old Cadillac that might or might not make it to Omaha. Her sister lived there with enough money in the bank that the two of them could make ends meet for a long time. That's what she knew she had to do, had to make ends meet, had to disconnect a beginning from an old middle that didn't know how to let go of anything. She knew that if I didn't stop hanging on to the face of a cliff that didn't exist, maybe I wouldn't ever exist either.

She could *visit* my sisters and their kids, so she knew they existed. She said it right out: "I want to visit *you*." She said it standing there in the jeans she'd only recently learned to wear, the sleeveless blouse that revealed her still-pretty arms, pushing her hair out of her face, squinting in the sunny Iowa wind as she filled that tank. That's when I walked into the little store looking for something good for myself, nonchalantly unfolding the bills she'd given me as if I'd ever done something that had cost me anything.

She was gone when I came back out, left me standing with an ice cold Coke in my hands in a parking lot somewhere east of Oskaloosa, where the Des Moines runs cold and southeasterly toward its big sister. I stood there a long time turning that bottle warm. The wind scraped hot over my skin, the cash in my pocket enough maybe for a few skimpy meals, but not enough for a room. A car whipped by every minute or so, like the questions rising in my head with an urgency I had never known.

I drank the last of the warm Coke, realizing that I should've bought her one, too. That was the crux of it, the crux of everything. Either way, it wouldn't have gone to waste. My thumb grew heavy in the air, brand new in its potential, knowing that it could take me anywhere but Omaha.

MUTATION

FULL

moon, I am listening. Your clean
sheet of music clarifies the sky.
The oaks of an old grove
thread this winter neighborhood
together above the roofs,
reach toward the mottled sheen

of your face. Simplified, full moon,
I walk this street so late
all the houses are full of bodies
breathing beneath the sheets,
your light reduced to dim blades
stretched across their floors.

Where the road ends, I step out
into the field, out into the grass,
out . . . into . . . the open, exposed
for what I am if not for whom.
Five deer, their backs on fire,
lift their heads and stare at me.

How many steps can I take how slowly,
to hold them on the edge of breaking?
It's either them or me, and they know it,
their ears flicking back for fellow voices,
then forward again to follow me

as tightly as their eyes.

                    Full moon,
I move so slowly now I remember . . .
ah yes, here I am, here it is . . .
ground . . . my feet . . . cold air . . . smoke
of breath . . . hands in readiness before me . . .
eyes returning eyes . . . dark circle
of wind-stripped trees around me . . .

DOLLARS

Children knock on my door,
claiming to have raked my maple leaves
for the fair price of one crisp dollar.
That's when I make up something good
to tell them. For example, the tale where
I cannot give them one of my dollars
because a giant ear broke into my house last night
and sucked up every noise,
even those beyond the range of human hearing,
and since everyone knows I navigate
by bite-sized bursts of sound
emitted by certain nose-hairs,
and since all my dollars flit around the house
like drunk moths, obviously
I cannot locate said dollars
and must accept aforementioned yard-raking
as a gift. There is nothing so beautiful
as the double-headed silence of two children,
unless it's the way their gazes
connect in disbelief. Still,
back they come almost every afternoon.
Yes, I'm certain I've lived far too long,
for some days after I've unraveled
some whopper about a giant rat, let's say,
who relishes the juicy eyeballs of children,

or some fiery-eyed horse with the wings of a dragon
and hooves of thunder,
I nevertheless drop one of my crumpled dollars
into each of their tiny palms.
No wonder they return, dumping
humongous bags of golden maple leaves onto my lawn
and raking them up again.
I fear every creased and rumpled dollar
in every room and pocket in my house
is doomed. For I pay the price of a good raking
again and again. The sound
of feet kicking up leaves
is as good as breathing deep—breathing long.

SALUTE

I caught up with a college kid
who lounged on a rock beside the trail.
He said the pack he carried
was a parasail, forty-five pounds.

Later, he caught back up with me
in the middle of eating an apple.
I cut him off a piece
and he chewed it slow.

The sun was ruthless,
not a single tree for shade,
just grass and wildflowers
hustling over the steep slope.

I passed him once more and made it
to the top of Jumbo Mountain
first. A windsock was full,
stretched tight as a pointing finger—

a sign, sure enough.
I found a spot clear of deer scat,
lay down with my pack for a pillow,
and surveyed Missoula

spreading west and north.
And to the east, the Rattlesnake
where I once met a brown bear face to face.
Finally the kid arrived,

dropped his pack, held an instrument
to the wind. "Too strong," he called
and sat down cross-legged in the grass.
I studied clouds: white continents

creeping over the south ridge.
When I woke up, the young man
was lighting a small pipe, puffs
of pot smoke—good smell

like sage when you break off leaves
and roll them in your hand.
An apple for a toke, or two,
I wanted to say, but didn't.

I would've thought charging
the edge of a mountain
to lunge into the spiral limbs of an updraft
would be enough to thwart one's

angle on the world. But is anything
ever enough for a skinny kid?
I waved as I started back past him.
He stood at attention and saluted.

When I was almost down the mountain
I saw him surface on the north-face horizon
like one of those clouds—making
great slow swoops over the slopes,

dangling like a ripe piece of fruit, a seed,
beneath the red blades of his wings.
Moments later he crashed at the foot of the trail
a hundred yards ahead of me.

I ran to help if I could, took a nosedive,
tumbled, came up scrambling. When I
reached him, he lay face-down in lupine,
his red sail snared in a bank of big sage.

Tangled in his harness, he shuddered
like something on the ground beneath him
was trying to break through.
He rolled over slowly. Blood

sputtered from his mouth. He smeared
his lips red with the back of his hand,
opened his eyes, and, when he saw me,
broke into glorious laughter.

THE NECESSARY

Nothing seduces like the wind
lifting up her skirts and passing overhead
among the whipped leaves and limbs,
that big-mouthed zone of swallows and crows,
lisping her two or three words
of prolonged astonishment.

Nothing is older or more necessary
than her spontaneous whirling
over the neighborhood, over the surrounding
forest veined with highways, over the burnished
windows of cities and the creature curves
of rivers and creeks, over
undiscovered caves beneath boulders,
over sand and bottomland and root
and rock, until her dance
subsides, the final vestiges
whirlwinds among the red and yellow leaves.

Nothing clarifies like the cold fingers
and shoulders of such a wind,
polishing you like a deep stone in the creek,
walking alone down the endless street.

OLD LISTENER

It seems like nothing will ever begin.
Spiders sleep under the maple leaves.
Cars have grown cold,
sinking into the ground.
The owls of Sandy Run
have turned their attention
to the succulence of small eyes.
Every patch of woods rings
with the memory of dogs.
One window casts its pale light onto grass.

Take all of it now
before it's too late,
before the sky becomes whole again,
new light pooling in the tops of trees.
Take the air uncurling over the pond,
take the bitter feet of the crows
holding on to their high part of the night,
take the crystalline breath of the fox
pulsing among small leaves
and the cold wide-open faces of trout
gathering in the deepest darkest water.

Take this body,
its hands two small birds
seemingly dead on the sheets,
its feet two white exclamations
wasted in the darkness,
this heart that has never learned
to rest unguarded,
this mind withdrawn
into its own voices.

I am asking you, old listener,
to come to the stillness of this room
if you are not here already.
I am asking you
to ease into these hands and feet,
pulling this body on like an old coat
that was made for you.
I am asking you to rise up and speak.

HUNGER IN A SMALL TOWN

Birds wear the last light on their shoulders,
huddle together on lines
holding the course of our voices in their feet.
From the upper floors of houses and apartments
we look into their islands of leaves.
They see only themselves in our windows
or else an opening into more green space.
A wren knocks herself out on my pane.
Head laid back, eyes clouded and half closed,
her wings tremble in the tall blades.
Who will get there first:
me or the cat or the rain?
Already she has surrendered.

ↄρ

I eat everything that is put before me
and ask for more
though the teachers of spirit have told me
you are drawn only to hunger.
In this town of prayers
that outnumber the leaves,
I listen for you in the measured beseeching,
I listen among the ringing of phones
and the one-sided words,
suspecting that you linger only

in empty alcoves.
So what are you doing in my house
wearing your silence like a thorn?
I hurl my words into every corner.
Still, in unguarded moments,
you enter my pores,
you travel inside me like my blood.

*

The gray fox and the rat
skulk along the drainage ditch,
each on that ancient mission.
I hunker on my mound of warm red clay,
hiding among the limbs dipping low,
and listen to the small waters,
the small trafficking of natives
below the wind of cars.

*

There are patches of warm air in the pastures
where horses stroll.
An oak struck by lightning
is broken over the old shed row,
its branches segmented over the ground

like a thought interrupted,
the stalls full of spiders and collapsed walls.
When the last forked branch
has sunk into the ground like a fading pulse,
there will still be the breath of a horse
and the white morning sky of fields.
Even now a cloud of juncos
hovers in the space that was once that oak,
almost taking its shape for a moment,
before dropping into the tall grass.

꿁

The doors downtown
open and close like barnacles
in the wash of a rising tide.
October is cold even here at first light.
The air, though it surrounds and touches everywhere,
though it enters our bodies enriching our blood,
has never been enough.
The routines of our homes and offices and construction sites
have never.
The light working its way down the branches,
down the stones of the church on the hill,
has never.
Our prayers shedding themselves of us on the cold ground

and rising into the constellations
have never.
Wherever you are—
wing-maker,
drinker of bone marrow,
conductor of wind and water,
swallower of wars and all their witnesses—

we are waiting.

THE KEYS

1.

The engine starts back right away,
but turning around in this place is
impossible, and backing up, a discipline
of years. I kill the engine
and darkness pours
into the hole my lights had made.
An owl blinks vision back into his brain.
Moonlight trickles down through leaves.
My keys nestle in my palm
and make a clinking sound like coins
going into my pocket.

2.

Waiting in the woods' edge
I hear the buck wandering alone
through fallen leaves and branches.
Once I saw him at dusk
turning to stare
into the yellow glare of sun,
rack ridiculous with size and weight,
a small tree sprouting
from that empty mind of grazing
under the moon. Later,
in that instant of lowering

his head to the dark pond,
he saw the curse that will draw
a bullet to his heart.
Erased it with a drink.

3.
Far out at the center the silver flash of something
not a fish—my keys. The circles begin again,
sliding over the surface toward the certainty
of weeds and banks . . . one answer I have given
to myself, standing on the ground
with empty pockets and empty hands.

THE ORIGIN OF MOUTHS

My parents called it nightmare.

I called it fear—
the way exhaustion took my hand
and led me down gray hallways
into the presence of

mouths,
a forest of them not attached to faces,
opening and closing—but why?

And when I woke shouting
into my room bisected
by the razor sheen of moonlight,
the faces of my parents and sisters—
whole faces complete with eyes—
hovered over my sweat-soaked bed.
Behind them in the fabric
of co-mingling darkness and light
the mouths still pulsed,
stunning my brain into silence.

Today, forty years later,
as I hike up this canyon of Capitol Reef,
enjoying equally the raw heat of noon
and relief of canyon shade,

I recognize those mouths
in the chaotic skull of a colossal stone—
unmoving now, but open,
the elemental idea of mouths
and all their purposes,
emerging out of the cavern
of time before words.

LISTENING TO THE
WHITE-THROATED SPARROW

three held notes
keen as a penny whistle
the fourth a shimmering tremolo
that rides the late glare of the lake

then sidles through corridors
of birch and maple
sliding over the hillside
like windblown mist

the singer so patient
that the silence that follows
swells like unfurling fists
in the hollow dens and coverts

while those four notes
stack up in that sturdy
flick of a body
and then come falling again

over these Virginia woods and spines
stalling me like a dry leaf
that stays afloat but spins and descends
the rifts of white water

MUTATION

1.
Before I can get out the door
my mother shows up
to polish my birdfeeders
as if they were fine wooden boxes
or maybe her dead father's wingtips.

She tells me about the times
she sailed on the lake as a child
in a raft she made from inner tubes and old planks,
the summer breeze filling her sheet,
pulling her out to the end of a long cord like a kite.
Her father on the tree-lined shore was her audience,
she said. She lay down flat on the raft and tried
to open her eyes sideways like a lizard.
She learned how to hang off the edge
and fish with her paw like a bear.
And sometimes she would stand tall, balanced
on one foot, a joker's silhouette against the lake's
reflected light—her father applauding
and whistling from the shore.

When I come back late
the birdfeeders are so full of seed and cardinals
and bluejays and woodpeckers and titmice
the limbs droop toward the ground, the birds
so busy fending each other off they forget to eat.

2.

The gray clouds of cats lurk
within the blooming wisteria nearby.
My mother cultivated feral tabbies like these
underneath the toolshed of the house I grew up in.
They took over the yard, the neighborhood,
the patch of woods at the end of the street.
In those days she occupied herself all day
by keeping them off the birds with such
complexities of vigilance her eyes would glow.

She has gone back to her apartment now,
comfortable in her lounge chair,
watching animal behavior on TV,
but I know what she expects of me.
I'm supposed to creep across the lawn
on all fours like a giant spider,
a mutation so bizarre that all the world
must stop to witness, the fluid bodies of cats
grown solid as ceramic in the underbrush
while the birds cock their heads from the lips
of feeders and chip their warnings on the air.
If she were here she'd be standing on that porch,
smiling, but no whistles or applause
that would frighten the birds and cats.

It's your strangeness that holds the world
at bay, she'd say. Keep your mind busy
with stalking. Hold the cats and birds in balance.
Look into their eyes, study them,
keep their hunger alive.

THE AMBUSH GARDEN

I spoke into the empty room
and called it song, although
it had no tune, no rhyme,
and worse, I was moved by my words
that reached no one else—moved

to walk up the street and see everyone
conducting their energy like newborn
fuses, to sit in the bookstore lounge chair
and hear the characters under dust jackets
chanting mantras. After that,

whatever changed, whatever shifted—
even a face rising into view like a white flute
in the hands of a precocious child
on the verge of blowing over the open hole—
drove my heart out of its ambush garden.

What we hope almost never makes
its presence known, except for that day
when all the thought-leaves fall
to the ground—then the limbs, then
the trunk, gnarly roots gasping for air.

Then something new begins to coalesce
in that stump-hole, the unfamiliar face of what
we really know, showing each profile,
the back of the head, the mystery of its
full frontal gaze. Why am I speaking to you

in this way? You are the knowing hands
touching the flute holes of awakening
wood, the face flickering through levels
of light. But what does that mean to anyone
but me, the one who opens the door, stares

into the vacant space for a moment, and then
speaks as if I know anything beyond the rising
of one moment on the back of the last one,
or is it falling, or sliding sideways behind
the maple tree in a garden of endless mirrors?

OPEN HOUSE

One Sunday morning we drive
to Famous Anthony's as usual.
I have my regular pancakes
and you the French toast with bacon.
As we eat, silence gathers
between us like twisted sheets
asking, "Is this all there is?"

We look into each other's faraway eyes
and know that this day calls
for the paper's list of open houses.
Here, among the sticky remains
of breakfast, we find the promise
of doors opening to us
at 1 p.m., 2 p.m., 3 p.m., and 4.

We rush home and put
our own house in order.
We dress in fresh jeans
and collared shirts. We look
into each other's eyes and know
the time has arrived.
We climb into our old Honda
and crank up the radio and the heat.

The 1 p.m. is *a must see to believe.*
We see and we believe— hardwood
floors and ceiling fans, front porch
rockers and a staircase winding to a master
bedroom loft. Looking down on the dark
conversation pit, we know the dog
would struggle with that corkscrew climb,
that we would talk and talk and talk.

The 2 p.m. is *a fixer-upper priced 2 sell.*
Layers of wallpaper, like the rings
of ancient trees, tell the weather
of earlier times, the taste of the long-dead.
We see our future spread before us:
stripping walls, painting, living in a backyard
tent to rip up floors and gut the baths,
to face the ever-changing challenges of tile.

The 3 p.m. is *acreage with a barn*
and fenced pastures. Plateaus
of cow shit harden in the cold wind.
A rusty horseshoe announces each threshold
inside and out. The ranch-style house
lies like a closed eye in the treeless pasture.
We sit on a plank of plywood and lean together,
imagining emaciated horses trotting in a ring.

The 4 p.m. is our *dream come true,*
if by dream they mean a studio and a rose garden
and a house that is a universe unto itself.
Weathervanes cruise among the clouds.
Closets reveal hidden stairs and secret wormholes.
Lost in the spiraling galaxy of the third floor
where rooms orbit us like unknown planets,
we have to use our cell phone to call for help.

The winter afternoon is turning dark
as we head home. The silence
that drove us to other houses
transforms to quiet now, hand
in hand above the console.

We park in our driveway and stay
in our seats for a moment, listening
to the wailing of Bob Dylan,
and then to the wind. We savor the call
of warm lights shining in our windows.
Our dog behind the fence grows impatient,
breaks the crystal air
with her abrupt versions of our names.
We have seen enough
from the list of open houses
to know who we are once again,
and who we'll never be.

NEW ANIMAL

The skull of my dog
when I take her face in my hands;
the wet, black pupils of her eyes
that look into mine, searching,
until they switch toward the sound
of the postman on the stoop.
He leaves a batch of envelopes
that I'll tear open for those inner
pages that tell me what I have
to pay if I am to continue
being in this place.

The finger of my neighbor's infant,
sticky with spit and grainy
with remnants of her chocolate chip
as she touches
the corner of my mouth, my open
eye, the half shell of my ear.

The voice of Harriet resonating
with our living room full of drums.
The tones of her Indian flute—
cedar and leather. They could fill
Bear Creek canyon where I once saw
three owls like whole notes opening
and closing their gold eyes

on a limb hanging low
over the trail.

        The limb of the tree
I walked out on as a boy, balancing
high over the neighborhood
where my neighbors gathered at dinner
that evening in their tidy homes. My eye
traveled through the tops of old oaks
and maples planted for their fall colors
to the edge of the woods
and into the nest of a red-tailed hawk.
She raised her head and looked at me
as if I were some new kind of animal
that may not know of fragile things.

GOYA'S DOG

The body of Goya's dog is lost
behind the horizon of a hill.
Her head rests on that line
like a risen moon, risen
because she's looking forward
into the vast open space
of ascending hills; and because
she's looking upward into
the openness of unlimited sky.
Her mind the essence of not knowing,
she loves that there is so
much to explore. She cocks
her head and listens to the wind
voicing its concerns over
the ridges, sending its perfect
desire to exist into the folds
of these rolling hills. She cocks
her head the other way and sees
the plover flickering from point
to point in the grass. She drops
her nose to the dewy scruff
and draws into her brain
the trail of a fierce grouse hen
and her scurrying brood.

I choose to ignore what science
says about dogs, that they
don't feel what we feel—
love, grief, gratitude,
loneliness, joy. Likewise
I choose to ignore what
religion says about dogs,
that they have no soul, no
continuous spark of connection
to the divine. I ignore
because I know they are only
protecting their territories—
the way a dog comes flying
out from under the porch
to chase away anyone
who dares get too close
to the sacred yard—making
their comfort zones into dogma.
Liberated from our need
to prove and be right,
from our will to assert
and control, Goya's dog rises
full-bodied on the horizon
like a shadow rippling
over the blazing earth,
driven by hunger and thirst

and ferocious pleasure.
Dwelling fully in her body
and soul, she trots off
and disappears into the grass,
reappears on a distant hill, heading
purposefully for the nowhere
becoming the somewhere
beneath her feet, ready
for whatever these knolls and ridges
offer her.

SAYINGS OF AN OLD SLASH PINE

1.
When needles whisper,
horizons climb from the hourglass
of the black widow's belly,
stretch out their wings to dry in the sun,
and undertake their long
migrations over the land.

2.
If your brothers hover,
if your sisters shiver,
it was fire that made earth ready,
that sacrificed oak and maple.
It stretches under the bed of brown needles
like a laugh.

3.
When your cones perch among birds
that blab and shit all day,
when they spread their keeled scales
to expose the hidden twins,
you will yield the dust of your desire
and the wind shall go everywhere.

4.
If salt water
rises into the slash
where you sleep
and stalls your yellow spore
in pools that harden under the sun,
remember that your seeds have wings.

5.
What you exude
under the shawl of night
will shine on the bootsoles of hunters.
If the dog's bark bounds
through the hole of the sun,
you are growing in the heartwood of a man.

6.
When the final instar
fastens its claws in your bark,
sacrifice your twigs to its eggs,
seize its song,
and the young shall fall into the soil
and feed upon your roots.

7.
Not even the stars
know
if it is you
that clutches earth
or earth
that clutches you.

BREAKING THE SAGE

1.
Chico sips his coffee, won't say anything
to me. All day, I follow him from street corner
to parking lot to park bench to McDonald's,
watch him begging with a plastic cup
and a pair of rhythm spoons on his knee.
All night his face watches me in my dreams.
My wife says I lost my mind when I lost
my job at the bottling plant. Her waiting
tables keeps a low noise rumbling under the rugs.
My little boy licks faces on the tube and dials
a crow on the wire outside his window.
One, one, one, one, one, one, one.
Meanwhile, a TV man in plastic glasses
pulls the trigger and tiny birds explode.

2.

A door opens and shadows flap through.
Discarded butts still smoke on the floor
and somebody's passing a bottle of wine.
A dog lies down on a sleeping child.
I follow my thoughts into outer space,
then follow them back into Chico's eyes.
He sits on a rug under focused light.
He rolls a cigarette and licks it clean.
I would close the door and shut them all in
but he promises the knowledge of gods, and I
can't leave. So I crawl to a corner and make
myself small as the head of a mole. Chico
works the room with his hat held out.
He's taking donations for a new set of wheels.

3.

Chico picks me for his wilderness pilgrimage.
My wife says don't bother to come back.
The sky is unmarked and the radio plays
cowboy songs that make me ask questions.
Will I ride a long trail, will I sleep under stars?
I think of my boy, how he runs to me
whenever I call. How can you leave him,
she said. The land out here is a great gray brain
and I'm the husk of a thought caught
in the sage. If Chico doesn't wake I'll just
keep driving. I love this old engine that won't
make it a week. How can he sleep inside so much
noise? The wind slaps in through broken
glass. Chico's face is an old brown hat.

4.

I've given him money and a pair of red socks,
the palm of my hand with its decipherable lines,
a belt that's too big, the smooth lucky rocks
I found in a mountain creek, cheap wines,
a recycled voice that gnaws on old bones,
the tendency to swallow when I'm being observed,
a stained white jacket with the zipper gone,
the love of a wife and child that was undeserved.
I've taken his laugh and his empty stare,
the back of his hand on the front of my face,
his dirty fingernails and his lunatic hair,
his ranging through streets at a drunken pace,
and I'll keep on taking till he tells me to stop.
If this is a test, then I'm not giving up.

5.

The woman smiles and Chico takes her hand.
A white half moon burns over the bay.
Back in the room Chico slakes his need
for fusion. I follow the sidewalk into old
avenues and look into gallery windows. A bench
in the nightshade of a cottonwood is empty
and I place myself there ceremoniously.
Questions stretch out in my veins:
What does Chico want from me?
Answer: money, food, a driver.
What do I want from him? Answer:
It feels good to have nothing and walk a step
behind. Answer: I want him to pull the plug
in my head and let me drain. I want to be free.

6.

Chico stands on a cement table and preaches
ghosts, how they follow sparks of light,
wear necklaces of dead white leaves,
their voices tumbling in the dirt. How
we can't hear them with the soles of our feet
which are covering the miles or baring their
featureless faces to the moon. A child
my son's age isn't listening. She kneels
to study the wind in trash. Turns
to the rush of swallows raiding the air.
Someone coughs, someone takes out keys.
Chico is a small storm in a vacant rest stop.
There was no laughter in their hands, he says.
Not one of them could hear me or see me, he says.

7.
I lie on the ground and cover my eyes.
The white clouds hold fire, and the flies
circle scat. The food ran out three days ago.
We picked up a dog, but it took off
when the moon turned bright. Chico's cough
is making blood. We find a back road and park,
lay blankets down next to the bald tires.
I stopped naming the days and forgot my wife's face.
There's nothing new or old we can't throw
in the ditch. We study the disappearing arc
of a star, dismantle our thoughts like chicken wire.
New skills: I can hold shoes on my feet without laces,
and walk all day in the knowledge of this:
wherever I feel like it, I can take a good piss.

8.

We've holed up in this draw for over a week.
I don't plan to leave till he gives me a reason
to go home—the roots, maybe, of his own ruined eyes.
His words are black beetles in the dry weeds,
his hands dead sticks the wind broke loose
making shadow-shapes of crows and mustangs.
His scabbed-over feet slap on the rocks like mud.
Like a boy with his father, I make too much
or too little of him. I crawl his tracks,
lounge on a limb above his closed face.
The car died in Bridger a month ago.
I've been eating red berries and throwing them up.
Chico eats air and insects and leaves.
I can see his bones when the wind blows right.

9.

What am I doing here under this moon?
Three scorpions glide by the ball of my foot.
A rattlesnake taps my cheek like a dream.
Chico tracks faded prints in the sand.
His face and hands shine like burnished stone.
He circles back to me with the meat of a hare.
I have no power to speak or to move.
The sky lies down heavy against my eyes.
Stands of big sage clatter in the wind.
My body is sinking in the earth's undertow.
My brain crawls away like two lizards in the night.
Chico studies my eyes for the causes of life.
Far away, my son cannot sleep in his bed.
I can see it, the wild horse in his eyes.

10.
I woke up yesterday and Chico was gone.
Left no sign on the sandstone slab where he slept.
For so long I watched him without one word.
He found soiled sheets in an outfitter's camp,
washed them in a creek with fist-sized stones.
Dried them out on ivory rocks in the sun,
cut them with his knife, sewed them with saved-up
needle and thread. Made pants and a shirt.
Then he lay submerged in the creek like a bunch
of white sticks. Stood up naked in the canyon-light.
Put his new clothes on and burned the old.
He sang and danced around the flames. Today I start
my long walk home. This thinking alone tastes good.
I break off sage and breathe it in. I breathe it out.

NIGHT, AND THE MOCKINGBIRD

The girl presses her forehead to the mirror.
Cold glass draws away the heat. She stares
into the blurred reflection of her eyes
and finds green hills, the sky full of gray
and scarlet, grain fields displaying the body
of wind. Her feet touch down on a brown path
between meadows of gladioli and heather.
Light streams from the cracks in an old shack.
The knotty pine door swings open

and a mockingbird rushes to greet her
dressed in coveralls made of birch bark,
pressing stray strands of gray feathers
into place on her sleek head. She holds
the girl at wing's length and looks her over.
Leads the girl to a chair, pulls her long black
hair back from her face, presses forefeathers
into the girl's temples until a song
opens inside her skull, croons down the long
tuning forks of her bones. The bird strokes
the girl's forehead to form the furrowed brow,
the contours of surprise and poise and desire.
Then she takes the girl's face in her wingtips
to fashion the reverie-mask of solitude.

The mockingbird's own face roils, tornado
in a jar, her shiny black eyes the two craziest days
of summer. Carousel polkas fly from her mouth,
make fun of the voices that try to define the girl—
the mother's moodiness, the father's caustic wit,
the brother's bravado, the sister's sass. The bird's
mock voices penetrate the girl's stunned heart until
she stands, pirouettes, dances for only herself.

She wakes in the face of her mirror,
draws back until her eyes clarify again—
light blue as always, but somehow darker now,
as if the feathered night has nested in her veins.
Outside her bedroom window, the cloudless
moon waxes above a skein of limbs
where the mockingbird sings.

WHAT YOU KNOW

(In memory of Jerry Phillips)

It sounds crazy, but I lost track of my best friend.
We didn't live close to each other, but we
sometimes met halfway and traveled to the coast
or the mountains. We'd sit across from each

other and argue philosophy, religion, politics.
My emails, phone messages, and last resort
snail mail to him all went unanswered
for months. My queries of mutual friends

led nowhere. At last I took a day off
and drove to my friend's city only to find
his house abandoned and occupied
by a band of feral cats, no forwarding address.

Heading back home, exhausted, I pulled
off the road and parked among weeds, thinking
my friend did not want to be found,
not by me anyway. I wondered what

I had done to cause him to leave without
a word: something I said in a letter taken
the wrong way, that must be it. But how could I
correct this mistake now that I couldn't

find him? I woke up in the middle
of the night full of the absence of my friend's
remarkable face, his furrowed brow, the bulbous
nose, the wit of incredulity always lurking

behind those pale blue eyes. I was sick
with the absence of my friend's dismissive
hand gestures, the sketchbook in his lap, his tales
of Egypt and the God Horus, the fierce stubbornness

of his opinions, his generosity with money
and his disturbing portraits. I had fallen asleep
in my car, and I rolled the window down
for a breath of night air. A pair of owls called

deep in the woods. The light of a cloudless full moon
lay down on the lined highway like the bankless
body of a river. By that light, I saw
my friend standing in the middle of the road

with his head cocked to one side, his clothes
hanging old and worn on his body, his eyes full
of tears at the sight of his own lost friend. I blinked
and blinked, and he disappeared like a possum

scuttling into underbrush. I want this to be a night
like that one, old friend, only better, with you really
showing up on my doorstep in such glorious light
after a long journey to a place my inquiries

cannot reach. Please come in and sit down
in the best chair, have a drink of the best whiskey
money can buy, and report on what you've seen.
Criticize me, please. Tell me what you know.

STUDY

Study the hair on the back of your hand
    in light from the windows of a house
    you have purified with burning sage
Study the smoke rising into corner cobwebs,
    sliding over windows and framed photos,
    gathering over the unsuspecting dog
Study the sleeping dog, the twitch of her lips,
    the twinges of her limbs and eyes,
    the way dream rules her body even in sleep
Study your own dream, the way it plucks you
    from the river of your waking thoughts
    and drops you on a street lined with trees
Study the street you are following, no sign of cars,
    wind blowing in the high canopies
    where the candle of your father's face flickers
Study your own face in the mirror, a little like his,
    then move on quickly, close a door and another
    door, before the mystery engulfs you like the day
Study the day that drags its edges over the ground,
    that chases the new night before it
    and retreats from the old night at its rear
Study the night that holds no grudges, forgetting
    all that came before and goes after, licking
    the earth's fur like the mindless grooming of a cat
Study the cat who studies the sparrow on the feeder
    on the tree outside your picture window,

so still the wind gathers in its matted fur
Study the sparrow, the alert flick of its tail,
 the momentary black fixation of its eye,
 the gray seed twirling in its beak
Study the fixation of your studying, the way you fold
 inward, the way your thoughts and observations
 rise and fall like answers in an eight ball
Study the way those phrases sink back into darkness
 as delicious and necessary as a kiss,
 as searing as the fire that breathes in an old scar
Study your breath, the way it slows and turns at the top
 and again at the bottom, and again and again,
 the way it deepens shyly under your gaze

WOLF

I thought I'd tell you
that the day is bulging under the horizon

like the bubble emerging from the lips
of a sleeping child

and that behind this bubble
is another, turning and rising

out of a depth of fire
and wind and darkness and light

and that behind this is another
and that each of these days

has about it a blankness
that is both surprising and frightening

and for that reason
we become the hired or the hiring,

husband or wife,
predator or prey.

I thought I'd remind you
that we have made it all up

and that the days could be anything
if we would leave them alone.

Let's leave this day alone.
Let's all just stay where we are

and let the eye of one day crawl over us.
Don't speak, don't eat or drink,

don't dream of small or great victories.
Would God's one remaining wolf

crawl out from under the house
where he has been hiding all these years

and devour us all in our moment of weakness?
Would the bubbles of our days

rising out of the great sea that surrounds us
stop breaking on the surface of this world?

ETERNAL HOUSE

Oak leaves blow over the wide porch.

Windows stained by storms reflect
the low autumn sun.

Doors older than empires swing open.
Children scatter like cockroaches,
turn and rise up on their hind legs
when cornered, then shout as they run
into the garden.

A woman carries a tray of bread and wine
into the crowded dining room, all the names
carved into the long table, some long-buried
and lost under the names of others.

Mice skulk under the polished floors.
The bones of saints and murderers breathe
all night within the foundation, interior walls
morphing from stone to mud to brick to board.

The heads of beasts hang in a lighted hall
beside diplomas and awards. Books lounge
on the shelves hiding caches of the long dead
between the walls: diamonds, manuscripts,
diaries, loaded guns, rolls of cash, bloodied knives . . .

The widow's small room collects statuettes
and candles. An old dog curls up against
the crack of light, noticing through its lids
the late-night shadows of feet passing by.

In the kitchen cupboard, bags of flour and sugar
and salt stand at attention in their long rows.

In halls and bedrooms, closets harbor
abandoned staffs and clubs. Dresses cascade
into the rubble of footwear. Ties lap up
the darkness of overcoats and scarves.
Tickets to an old drama on the honor
of a daughter and her father the king nestle
in the breast pocket of a jacket. Belts
curl up like the rings of a bristlecone pine.

This is where I live. The past
grins at me from mantles. The dark brews
of the cellar lie in wait, still as the minds
of sages. Chameleons sprawl on window screens
like notes pinned to the lapels of lost children.
The glassed-in back porch embraces the best
winter sun, reserved for heads of the household.

I could take up hammer and saw,
apprentice myself to carpenters and architects—
build more rooms of mud and stick and brick
and stone and board and glass and steel.
I could take up the sword, the gun, the hand
grenade and defend the boundaries of the estate.

I could cook and serve meals. I could sit back
in the drawing room, prop my heels up
on good leather, smoke a cigar.
I could gather round the kitchen table
and sing. I could start an argument
or press my ear against the door and dream
the right weapon in my hand.

I could bear the new child in my womb,
bring her forth in white sheets.
Could withdraw from the pale husk of my body
in that same bed, with the hand of that child
on my face, her eyes beseeching me to stay.

I could stop everything, stand in the middle
of this empty, ancient house, listening
to the creaking of floor boards, the rattle
of windows in the wind, the satisfying rub
of tongue within groove. I could walk out

to the front field with the great tarantula
of the sky turning over my head, a moment
so naked and so long the house disappears,
its elements flying out into the bodies of trees,
the tall wild grass, the deer and the fox and the beetle.
I gaze out into the world from the porch of my own brow,
this house of my own making, and my undoing.

EPILOGUE

NAKED

I dream I am naked under moonlight.
I stand in my yard, white lizard on a stone.
Great shadows of trees and parked cars

curl up at my feet like dogs and sleep.
A summer breeze slides through maple leaves.
Light lies down like a thin sheet of water on the road.

A car drives by and people stare at me
through the window, mouths agape like seashells,
but I feel no shame or shyness.

I stand as if fresh from creation,
my feet the flesh of lilies in the grass.
My hands intuitively know each other

and fly like Luna moths around my face.
My body is just now discovering itself,
and thus no longer dreams of the passage of time,

its tennis shoes and tied-back hair,
its t-shirt selling beer and a rock band,
its hands rising to grasp and point.

I realize my nakedness is deeper than skin,
more than tiny hairs springing up in the breeze:
I can feel the wind-carved horse of my desire

waking up in my untethered, unadorned body.

BIOGRAPHICAL NOTE

JIM PETERSON is the author of six collections of poetry, three chapbooks, and a novel, *Paper Crown*, published by Red Hen Press and recently made available on Audible. His collection *The Owning Stone* won Red Hen Press's Benjamin Saltman Award for 1999. His newest collection, *Speech Minus Applause*, was released by Press 53 in February of 2019. His poems have appeared widely in journals including *Poetry, Georgia Review, Shenandoah, Poetry Northwest, Prairie Schooner, Sugar House Review,* and *Cave Wall*. His stories have appeared in the *Los Angeles Review, South Dakota Review,* and *The Laurel Review*. A collection of stories is forthcoming from Red Hen Press in 2021. Retired Coordinator of Creative Writing at Randolph College, he is on the faculty of the University of Nebraska-Omaha's Low-Res MFA Program in Creative Writing. He lives with his charismatic corgi, Mama Kilya, in Lynchburg, Virginia.